A STUDENT'S GUIDE TO

RESISTING

PragerU PROPAGANDA

from the editors of
CURRENT AFFAIRS

printed by Current Affairs, Inc. / ISBN 979-8-9888487-1-4

WHAT IS PragerU ?

PragerU calls itself "the largest educational media company the conservative movement has ever seen." Despite the name, they're not actually a university, but their videos have been viewed billions of times. They have produced thousands of hours of content, and are branching out into new formats, including books and magazines.

Lately, PragerU has been creating a lot of material for schools. Florida recently approved the use of PragerU videos in classrooms. Maybe your teacher has shown you one. Or maybe your parents make you watch them. If so, we'd like you to read this little guide, because we want to help you avoid believing things that aren't true. We want you to consume media with a critical eye that will help you become a thoughtful member of a democratic society. In a democracy, the people themselves have to make important decisions about politics, so you need to learn how to avoid being tricked by demagogues.

This is what you need to remember: **PragerU lies to you.** They are a propaganda outlet, totally uninterested in telling the truth. But they're good at what they do. PragerU says it recruits "the most sought-after production, design, and marketing staff from Hollywood and beyond."[1] Bringing in over 60 million dollars a year and operating out of a 40,000 square foot headquarters, PragerU's 100+ staff produce slick, engaging, highly professional content that can appear sensible and persuasive. If a PragerU video is your first exposure to a topic, you may think it sounds pretty reasonable. Or, even if you know that it's biased, you might not know precisely *how* it's wrong, and if someone asks you to explain why it's wrong, you would find it hard to pinpoint the exact problem.

We're here to help. ***Current Affairs*** is a political magazine in New Orleans. We specialize in exposing bad arguments and showing why things that may *look* true are actually misleading or completely wrong. Our politics are the opposite of PragerU's, but the difference between us and them is that we commit ourselves to telling the truth. We present the arguments fairly, without resorting to wild distortions, so that you can make up your own mind based on a full understanding of the two sides' positions.

This guide is going to show you how PragerU distorts the truth and tries to get you to swallow conservative political ideology without realizing that it even *is* conservative political ideology. We hope that if you encounter PragerU material in your classroom, this guide will help you maintain a skeptical attitude toward it and see how it might be manipulating you.

REMEMBER: Don't take our word for any of this! Think for yourself.

Spotting Right-Wing Ideology

PragerU is **right-wing**, which means that its material endorses a particular set of controversial beliefs about the way the world is and ought to be. Here are some of the basic assumptions you'll see in their videos:

- Free market capitalism is the best economic system, and "socialism" will destroy society. Wealth inequality (some people being poor while others are rich) is not something we should object to.
- America is a land of opportunity where any inequality can be transcended if you work hard enough. Inequality faced by Black people (or any historically marginalized group) is a result of a failure of personal effort rather than any systemic barrier that makes success harder to attain.
- Global warming is not actually that much of a problem, and those who argue we need major new action to stop it are exaggerating. Fossil fuels are good for the world and we should continue to use them.
- The "left" promotes a harmful set of cultural values, including feminism and tolerance of LGBTQ people.
- The United States is the greatest country in the world and the Founding Fathers' vision for the country should be followed rather than challenged. The U.S. military is an overwhelming force for good in the world and our use of military force is at best justified and at worst an unforeseeable tactical mistake.
- The country of Israel is unfairly singled out for criticism despite being a beacon of democracy and freedom.

As you watch PragerU videos, watch for examples of these messages recurring. Sometimes they are snuck in very cleverly! For instance, in a video about critical thinking, which is supposedly trying to teach you how to think independently, the *example* of "independent thinking" it uses is a student questioning the scientific consensus on climate change. It's perfectly fine, of course, to interrogate scientific findings. But notice that PragerU is choosing to encourage you to question *climate scientists* and not encouraging you to question, for instance, its own propagandistic videos.

The Aesthetics of
CREDIBILITY

This is just a fancy way of saying: PragerU looks like it knows what it's talking about, and sounds like it knows what it's talking about. But that doesn't mean it does! You might have heard the expression "If it looks like a duck, swims like a duck, and quacks like a duck, then it probably is a duck." And you might think that's just simple common sense. But maybe it's not. It might look like a duck, swim like a duck, and quack like a duck, but be nothing more than *a very convincing imitation of a duck*. PragerU videos look educational, they sound educational, they say they're educational, but they're not educational at all. (Unless you want to learn how propaganda works, or what the world looks like to conservatives.) Just because someone wears a lab coat, doesn't mean you should listen to their medical advice, and just because a video purports to come from a "university," does not mean it contains high-quality information that you can rely on to be true.

WEARING A TIE IS A WELL-KNOWN WAY OF MAKING YOURSELF LOOK LIKE YOU ARE CREDIBLE AND INTELLIGENT

"Smiling faces sometimes pretend to be your friend. Smiling faces show no traces of the evil that lurks within... Smiling faces tell lies."
— The Undisputed Truth (1971)

Not Everything Is What It Seems

It looks like a dog, walks like a dog, barks like a dog, but this is a Japanese man in a $15,000 dog costume that he bought because he wanted to pretend to be a dog.

See: "Japanese man who spent £12,500 on authentic dog costume reveals how his family feel about his new life as a collie," The Daily Mail (Aug. 14, 2023)

BEWARE BOGUS CHARTS!

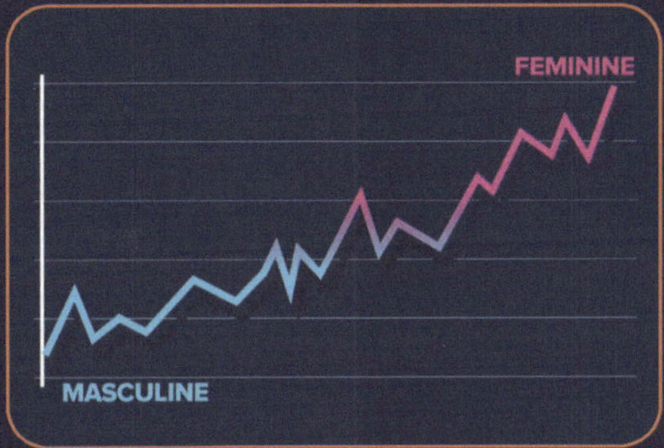

PragerU videos are chock-full of statistical data, charts, and graphs. But these are often pseudo-science and if you look closely you will notice they don't make sense, or parts of them aren't labeled, or it's unclear where the numbers came from. Read a book like Darrell Huff's *How To Lie With Statistics* to learn to spot common forms of manipulation.

Try naming some ways that these infographics are disastrously flawed.

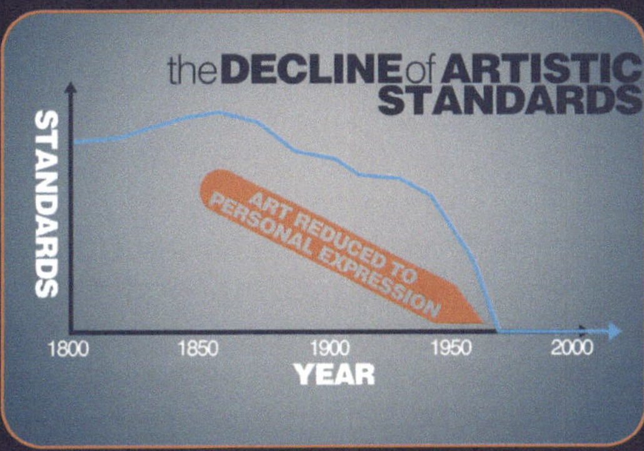

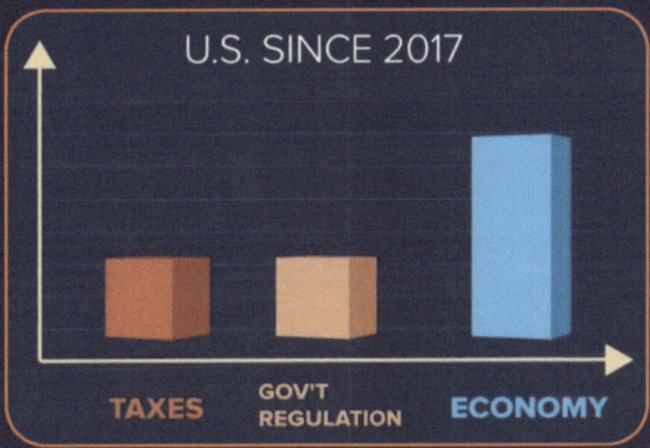

BEWARE PSEUDO-EXPERTS!

Expertise can be overrated. But PragerU's commentators often have affiliations with neutral-sounding organiztions like the "Independent Women's Forum" or the "Government Accountability Institute" that are designed to look like they do real research when they just pump out propaganda.

HOW TO SPOT PROPAGANDA

Propaganda is information designed to manipulate people's emotions, attitudes, opinions, and actions, often without their conscious awareness. It does this using lies and half-truths. For instance, during the time of Joseph Stalin's brutal rule in the USSR, a propagandist might have said: "Under the wise leadership of Comrade Stalin, the Soviet Union has transformed from a backward nation to a leading world superpower." This is not necessarily factually incorrect (the Soviet Union did industrialize and become a world superpower under Stalin), but leaves out the horrific mass murder and imprisonment that characterized his regime. Propaganda presents a selective picture of the world that can be emotionally powerful, and perhaps not even strictly *untrue*, but which ultimately intentionally distorts your understanding of reality.

Here are some examples of historical propaganda. Can you see how they were designed to manipulate the viewer? #1, the most innocent, is the kind of gentle manipulation found across advertising generally. Corn is "the food of the nation," a phrase meant to make you associate *being American* with *eating corn*. The picture makes corn seem wholesome and delicious. Perhaps it even makes you want a cornmeal pancake. In #2, the opposite technique is deployed: fear. Everything you love will go up in flames if the communists win! Right-wing propaganda is frequently fear-based, warning that terrible things will happen to civilization if, for instance, people are paid higher wages, or transgender people are accepted. In #3, a piece of Soviet propaganda, Joseph Stalin is made out to be a kindly father figure to the nation, even though he was actually a mass murderer.

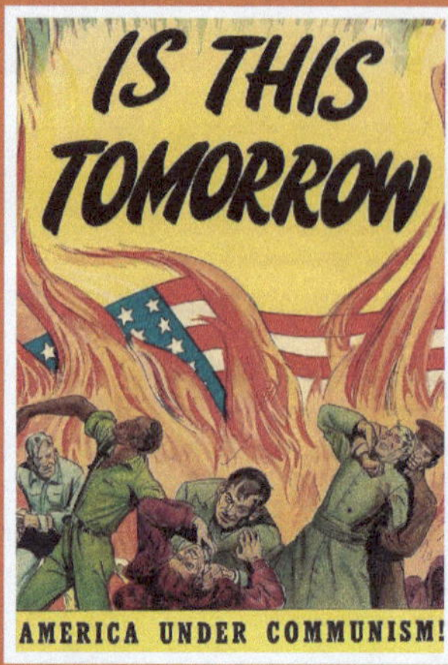

Most Soviet citizens probably didn't fall for this sort of propaganda, because they could see in their own lives just how brutal Stalin's regime was. But plenty of people outside the country were convinced by the false picture of Stalin that appeared in propaganda. In #4, we see a U.S. Army recruitment poster from World War I. Germans, instead of being portrayed as human beings, were depicted as a horrible "mad brute" who would kidnap women and attack America. Once again, fear was used to turn off people's brains. Finally, in #5, we see a piece of propaganda from Mao Zedong's China. The poster aims to make people feel like they are part of a great movement bringing a wonderful change to the country, with Mao hovering over it like the sun. The reality of Mao's China was just as grim as Stalin's USSR, but the poster successfully presses emotional buttons to get people to feel like Mao is leading them toward a great destiny.

AMERICAN MYTHOLOGY

PragerU simplifies complicated, flawed historical figures into mythical entities. Think about how figures like George Washington are being portrayed in their videos.
What is left out of the story?

On the right is an advertisement from *Claypoole's American Daily Advertiser* on May 26, 1796, offering a reward for the return of Ona Judge, an enslaved woman belonging to Martha Washington who ran away from the president's house in Philadelphia.[2]
Is Ona Judge mentioned in the video? If not, why do you think that is?

Ten Dollars Reward.

ABSCONDED from the houfehold of the Prefi-dent of the United States, on Saturday after-noon, ONEY JUDGE, a light Mulatto girl, much freckled, with very black eyes, and bufhy black hair—She is of middle ftature, but flender and deli-cately made, about 20 years of age. She has many changes of very good clothes of all forts, but they are not fufficiently recollected to defcribe.

As there was no fufpicion of her going off, and it happened without the leaft provocation, it is not eafy to conjecture whither fhe is gone—or fully, what her defign is ; but as fhe may attempt to efcape by water, all mafters of veffels and others are cauti-oned againft receiving her on board , altho' fhe may, and probably will endeavour to pafs for a free woman, and it is faid has, wherewithal to pay her paffage.

Ten dollars will be paid to any perfon, (white or black) who will bring her home, if taken in the city, or on board any veffel in the harbour ; and a further reafonable fum if apprehended and brought home, from a greater diftance, and in proportion to the diftance.　　　　FRED. KITT, Steward.

May 24　　　　　　　　　　　　　　3

TECHNIQUES OF
MANIPULATION
THE SELECTION AND OMISSION OF INFORMATION

Consider the following exchange:

INTERVIEWER: "Have you ever led a team of more than 20 people?"

CANDIDATE: "I've been involved with teams of over 50 people and played crucial roles in project management and coordination."

Did you notice that the candidate didn't directly answer the interviewer's question? We don't actually know whether they have led a team of more than 20 people. They presented information that gives the impression that they did, but it looks like they may have buried the fact that they did not, in fact, lead a team of more than 20 people.

You can create very misleading impressions on a listener by selecting which facts you present and which you omit! Consider the following quote from a PragerU video "What's Wrong With Government-Run Healthcare?"

"A second big problem with single-payer systems is that they are expensive—really expensive. A recent study by the Mercatus Center at George Mason University found that a Bernie Sanders-style 'Medicare-for-All' health system would cost a tidy $32.6 trillion over ten years."

$32.6 trillion sounds like a lot! But did you know that countries with "single-payer" healthcare systems (where the government, not private insurance, pays for medical care) actually spend *less* on healthcare than the United States?[3] You wouldn't know that if you watched PragerU, because they bury the information that doesn't fit with conservative political ideology.

When you're being made to watch a PragerU video, ask yourself questions like:

1. **What information am I not being told?**
2. **Whose voices am I not hearing?**
3. **What explains the decision to include/exclude certain facts or people?**

Here's an example from a PragerU Kids video. It's from *Craftory*, a series that combines teaching basic crafts with educational material. For instance, one video "celebrates American farms by making confetti eggs." The cheerful host relates some facts about farming in America while making the eggs and stuffing them with confetti. Most of the facts are banal. They are a little misleading (for instance, the host tries to portray contemporary farmers as "family-owned," downplaying the role of giant corporations in agriculture). But pay attention to this quote on the history of farming in America:

"Later into the 1700s, European settlers farmed across the 13 colonies. By 1790 almost all of American workers were farmers.

The following picture is displayed:

Can you spot the missing people and/or information?

That's right, the host neglects to mention that these "large plantations" were not being worked by families of "European settlers," but by millions of enslaved Africans, working under brutal conditions. The painting offers a romanticized view of American rural life that does not depict slavery.

Ask yourself that third question, then: Why was the decision made not to mention the role of enslaved people in working these farms? Well, because PragerU openly promises "pro-America content," and so it wants to tell an upbeat story about the country's history, minimizing such inconvenient facts as the genocide of Native Americans and the enslavement of Black people.

ACTIVITY: Write a PragerU Video

What information will you exclude? What information will you use? How will you make it seem like the left is evil, totalitarian, and wrong?

TIP: Conservatives often argue that there is a giant battle for the soul of civilization. So, for instance, PragerU believes there is a "war on boys," a "war on work," a "war on cars," and a "war on Christmas." These manufactured controversies are often called "moral panics." Why not make up your own phony war?

Fossil Fuels

Let's look at a specific, randomly selected PragerU video to see how viewers are manipulated using propaganda techniques into thinking conservative political ideology is true. This video is called "Fossil Fuels: The Big Picture," and it's hosted by Alex Epstein, author of a book called *The Moral Case for Fossil Fuels*. Epstein is challenging the view that the burning of fossil fuels (oil, gas, and coal) is causing harmful changes to the climate that require us to transition away from using them. Instead, he says, "the world needs more fossil fuels, not less."

Epstein says his argument is based on "eight essential facts." They are as follows:

1. **Cost-effective energy is essential to human flourishing.**
2. **Billions of people are suffering and dying for lack of energy.**
3. **Fossil fuels are uniquely cost-effective.**
4. **Fossil fuel energy neutralizes climate danger.**
5. **Global warming has been mild and manageable.**
6. **Warmer temperatures will save lives.**
7. **The "greenhouse effect" is a diminishing phenomenon.**
8. **Projected climate impacts can be managed with fossil fuels.**

Epstein claims that these facts, taken together, make the case for increasing rather than reducing fossil fuel use. He says that this is because they show that the benefits of fossil fuel use "outweigh the costs." This "cost-benefit analysis" means that even if fossil fuels cause some global warming, and global warming has negative effects, the upside of fossil fuel use is so positive that we should continue to use them.

It's important to think carefully about whether Epstein has in fact proven what he says he has proven. What do we make of this analysis?

A Quick Reminder of the Facts of Climate Change

Burning fossil fuels, such as coal, oil, and natural gas, releases significant amounts of carbon dioxide (CO_2) and other greenhouse gases into the atmosphere. These gases trap heat from the sun's rays inside the Earth's atmosphere, a phenomenon known as the greenhouse effect. As the concentration of these gases increases, more heat is retained, leading to global warming. Over time, this warming results in significant and often detrimental changes to global climates, causing sea levels to rise, extreme weather events to become more frequent, and ecosystems to be disrupted, which can have catastrophic consequences for both natural and human systems.

Fact 1

Fact 1 is basically irrelevant. Epstein points out that we depend on energy to power machines that improve our lives. An example he gives is incubators that keep babies alive. (Note the subtle suggestion that environmentalists will cause babies to die.) Those who advocate a transition away from fossil fuels believe that we need to move toward clean energy sources like solar and wind, that do not produce greenhouse gas emissions. They don't reject the idea that we need energy to power machines!

Fact 2

Fact 2 is irrelevant for the same reason. Epstein says that "Three billion individuals use less electricity per year than a typical American refrigerator. Most of them must use wood and animal dung to heat their homes and cook their food. To flourish, these people need far more energy." But it's not enough to show that many people need access to energy sources. For this fact to support Epstein's argument he would have to show that fossil fuels are the only energy source that could possibly satisfy their needs.

Fact 3

Fact 3 Epstein says: *"80% of the world's energy comes from fossil fuels. And fossil fuel use is still growing. The reason: nothing else can provide billions of people in thousands of places with low-cost, reliable, versatile energy. Unreliable solar and wind can't come close. They only provide electricity, which is just 1/5 of the world's energy use. And because solar and wind can go to near-zero at any time, they depend on 24/7 backup from reliable power plants—usually powered by fossil fuels."* But Epstein provides no data to support the contention that renewable sources can't *become* cost-effective. In fact, due to technological advances, renewable energy sources like solar and wind have seen dramatic cost reductions and are now competitive with, or cheaper than, many fossil fuels in many parts of the world.[4] Epstein just doesn't mention this, because he doesn't want you to know it!

Moreover, the *true* cost of fossil fuels should account for the harms of climate change itself,[5] and deaths from fossil fuel pollution.[6] Epstein mentions *none* of these harms.

Fact 4

Fact 4 Epstein says that deaths from climate disasters are "down 98% over the last century." Even if fossil fuel use causes global warming, he says, we can make up for the harms through inventions, like air conditioning, that protect us from the heat. But air conditioning isn't going to do much for those who are forced to work outside,[7] and if large parts of the Earth become outright uninhabitable, we're talking about millions of people having to uproot themselves find new places to live.[8]

Fact 5

Fact 5 Notice that Epstein says warming "has been" mild. *"While we're told that the warming we've experienced is rapid and overwhelming, the world has warmed just 1° C, 2° F since widespread fossil fuel use and CO2 emissions began in the 1800s."* But "just" is misleading. This is a huge change.[9] Furthermore, most of the damaging consequences are *yet to come*. It means nothing to say that the warming has been mild "so far" when the entire argument being made is that the worst consequences are still on their way!

Fact 6

Fact 6 Epstein says that more people die in cold weather than hot, meaning that warming should not be a problem. But even if this is true *now*, the effects of climate change that are bearing down on us are going to get worse over time! For instance, in Pakistan in 2022, unprecedented floods that were made worse by global warming damaged nearly 900,000 homes, killed over 1,000 people, and caused over $10 billion in damage.[10] These kinds of disasters are going to keep happening!

Fact 7

Epstein says that the greenhouse effect will eventually level off, and not keep getting worse indefinitely. But this is irrelevant to the argument for getting off fossil fuels, which is that *right now* the effect is going to continue to get worse, with catastrophic consequences.

Fact 8

This fact is essentially just a restatement of Fact 4. But Epstein gives a new example: he says that sea level rise could be contained through a system of water management like the Dutch use, and "the technology the Dutch use to keep the sea at bay is available to any country that needs it." But many countries are poor and can't afford to build elaborate new infrastructure.[11] In fact, one of the worst injustices of climate change is that its effects are going to fall hardest on the people who (1) did the least to cause the problem, because they burned the fewest fossil fuels and (2) have the least resources for dealing with natural disasters.[12]

So what does Epstein's case add up to? Nothing. It adds up to nothing. Remember, too, that he told us he was going to perform a "cost-benefit analysis" to show that using fossil fuels was, on balance, better than switching to renewable energy. But he didn't do that at all! First, he didn't actually show us that it was overly costly to transition to clean energy sources. Then, he didn't take into account or discuss most of the harms caused by fossil fuel use! 8 million people a year die from fossil fuel-caused pollution, a statistic unmentioned by PragerU.

A reminder of some of the harms of climate change left out of PragerU's "cost-benefit analysis":

Increased Frequency of Extreme Weather Events: This includes more intense hurricanes, typhoons, cyclones, wildfires, heavy rainfall leading to flooding, as well as prolonged droughts. We only need to look at the disastrous fires in Hawai'i to see how horrible these consequences can be for human beings!

Ocean Acidification: Increased CO2 leads to higher acidity in oceans, which can harm marine life, especially coral reefs and shelled organisms.

Loss of Biodiversity: Changing temperatures and habitats can lead to the extinction of many species that cannot adapt quickly enough.

Heatwaves: Increased frequency and intensity of heatwaves can lead to health problems, especially for vulnerable populations, and strain energy systems. Cities could experience hellish temperatures, making the mere act of breathing outdoors a suffocating ordeal, leading to countless heat-related fatalities.

Migration and Displacement: People will be forced to move from their homes due to sea-level rise, extreme weather events, or areas becoming uninhabitable due to heat or drought, leading to "climate refugees."

Spread of Diseases: Warmer temperatures can expand the range of many pathogens and vectors, like mosquitoes, leading to the spread of diseases like malaria and dengue fever.

Feedback Loops: Warming can lead to events that further increase warming, like the release of methane from melting permafrost, creating self-reinforcing cycles of increasing devastation.[13]

PragerU received over $6 million in start-up funding from, Dan and Farris Wilks, two billionaire brothers who made their fortune from fracking![14] Could this be part of the reason so many PragerU videos are devoted to claiming natural gas is awesome and the harms of fossil fuels are overstated?

Check The Sources!

PragerU videos have links to sources that supposedly support all of their factual claims. But often they don't! They look like well-sourced videos, but you need to check carefully to find out whether the sources are reliable and support the claims. Often, crucial information will be left out. For instance, to support Epstein's claim that "even extreme UN projections put [sea level] rise at 3 feet over the next hundred years," PragerU links to a Fox News story called "UN report on world's oceans is damning: 'We're all in big trouble.'"[15] That news report actually contains all kinds of information about how dangerous a rise in sea levels will be, quoting a vice chair of the IPCC and deputy assistant administrator for research at the U.S. National Oceanic and Atmospheric Administration saying that "the consequences for nature and humanity are sweeping and severe." It cites a warning from the United Nations Human Rights Council that a potential 'climate apartheid' could fracture the global population, splitting the planet between the wealthy and the rest of the world who will be 'left to suffer.'" Seems pretty important! Now ask yourself: WHY DIDN'T HE TELL YOU THAT INFORMATION? Answer: because he's a propagandist!

A Really, Really Bad Chart

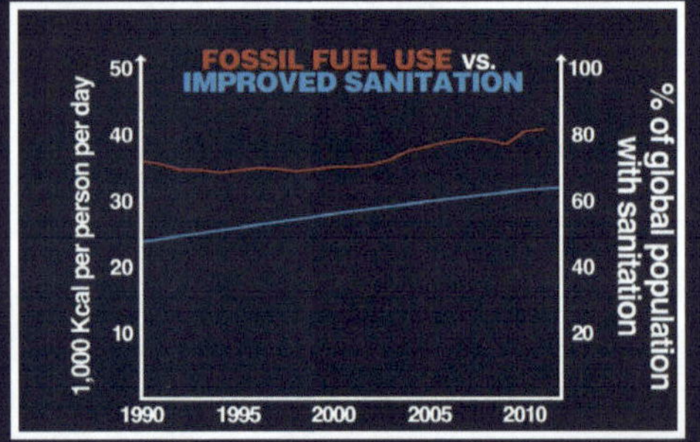

Q: PragerU uses this chart as part of its argument that we need to continue to use fossil fuels. Can you spot what's wrong with it?

A: A basic principle of statistics is that "correlation is not causation," which means that just because two trends occur together, it does not follow that one caused the other. The world abounds in "spurious correlations," phenomena that follow similar trends but aren't actually related. For instance, over the years, as margarine consumption has decreased, so did the divorce rate in Maine. But this doesn't mean eating less margarine strengthens marriages in Maine! For the above chart to make any contribution to Epstein's case, he would have to show that global sanitation use occurred because people used fossil fuels (and that sanitation can't be improved without fossil fuels). Of course, he doesn't show this. (For more on this kind of statistical mirage, see Tyler Vigen's book *Spurious Correlations*.)

"They Say Scandinavia, But They Mean Venezuela"

In this video, commentator Debbie D'Souza (who was born in Venezuela) argues that contemporary socialists want to replicate Venezuela's economic catastrophe in the United States, but dishonestly suggest that they want a Nordic-style social democracy instead. "The American left keeps telling us they want to take us to Stockholm," D'Souza says, "but its policies point in the direction of Caracas."

Very little evidence is provided for her position. She does not quote socialists. She does not go through the Bernie Sanders 2020 platform and show that it corresponds to Nicolas Maduro's legislative agenda.[16] That's because if she talked about the actual policies socialists are advocating (Medicare for All, a Green New Deal, paid family leave, workplace democracy), the Venezuela comparison would be laughable.

How does she do it, then? Well, there are a few familiar tricks that are pulled by conservatives when talking about Nordic countries. Sweden, Norway, Finland, and Denmark present difficulties for conservatives, because these countries are prosperous but also have "big government" programs and a strong welfare state, which destroys the conservative argument that "big government" kills the economy. (Norway, for instance, has far more public ownership than Venezuela![17]) Leftists like Bernie Sanders point to these countries to show that government-provided universal healthcare is not a pipe dream but a very feasible reality. D'Souza does not respond to that. Instead, she gives a common conservative talking point: actually, these countries are far more "capitalist" than Sanders will admit. This is because "most have private healthcare and education options," they "don't have a government-set minimum wage," and it's "easy to start a business."

All of this is extremely misleading. They're deliberately leaving out critical information. She doesn't tell you that private schools are virtually nonexistent in Finland's excellent education system.[18] Or that the reason there are no minimum wages is that unions are so strong that minimum wages are unnecessary.[19] Or that whether it is "easy to start a business" has nothing to do with socialism. She says these countries are "capitalist in wealth creation, socialist in wealth distribution," without noting the huge role the state plays in the economy itself.

So D'Souza's case only holds up because she selectively presents information calculated to mislead you. Why does she think socialists want America to look like "Venezuela"? Her only two arguments are that (1) in the Nordic countries, there are large Value Added Taxes, while the American left favors wealth and income taxes and (2) Venezuela introduced gun control. These are weak arguments. If the argument is that socialist policies will turn the American economy into the Venezuelan economy, gun control is essentially an irrelevant feature (Australia's gun control policies are strict, too.[20]) On taxes, it is hard to even grasp D'Souza's point. The Nordic countries do indeed have higher wealth, income, and inheritance taxes than we do, not just a VAT. There is just no evidence whatsoever that more taxes create a Venezuela-style economic crisis. There is, however, evidence that social democratic policies are correlated with happiness.[21]

Now try one yourself!

Look up every claim. Analyze every sentence. Scrutinize carefully. If you don't discover at least some manipulation or dishonesty, you probably haven't looked hard enough!

Leo and Layla is a PragerU cartoon about two time-traveling siblings who meet historical figures. Many of these videos are fairly innocuous and don't really have room for political "bias." (The Wright Brothers, Francis Scott Key, etc.) But sometimes, the videos are very clearly designed to push a conservative agenda, and give a misleading impression of history.

One of the most controversial Leo and Layla videos has been about Frederick Douglass, who escaped enslavement to become a great abolitionist activist, writer, and speaker. In the video, Douglass makes clear that slavery is wrong, but he treats the acceptance of legal slavery as kind of necessary evil that could not have been avoided by early Americans:

"I'm certainly not OK with slavery, but the Founding Fathers made a compromise to achieve something great: the making of the United States."

Nowhere in the video does it mention that most of the prominent founders, including George Washington, Thomas Jefferson and James Madison, personally kept people enslaved. In reality, while Douglass always insisted that the Constitution itself was a "glorious liberty document," he was utterly scathing about the hypocrisy of the American rhetoric of freedom. In a famous address called "What to the Slave is the Fourth of July," he argued that the early United States had no right to call itself a free country:

What, to the American slave, is your 4th of July? I answer; a day that reveals to him, more than all other days in the year, the gross injustice and cruelty to which he is the constant victim. To him, your celebration is a sham; your boasted liberty, an unholy license; your national greatness, swelling vanity; your sounds of rejoicing are empty and heartless; your denunciation of tyrants, brass fronted impudence; your shouts of liberty and equality, hollow mockery; your prayers and hymns, your sermons and thanksgivings, with all your religious parade and solemnity, are, to Him, mere bombast, fraud, deception, impiety, and hypocrisy—a thin veil to cover up crimes which would disgrace a nation of savages. There is not a nation on the earth guilty of practices more shocking and bloody than are the people of the United States, at this very hour.[22]

PragerU videos frequently encourage us not to "judge" those who committed horrible acts in the past—probably because if we did, it would make a lot less sense to venerate the Founding Fathers and commit ourselves completely to following their vision. Leo and Layla also travel back in time to meet Christopher Columbus, and at one point have the following interesting exchange:

LAYLA: *What about slavery? [...]*

COLUMBUS: *...Slavery is as old as time and has taken place in every corner of the world, even amongst people I just met. Being taken as a slave is better than being killed, no? I don't see the problem."*

LAYLA: *Well, in our time we view slavery as being evil and terrible.:"*

COLUMBUS: *Ah, magnifico! That's wonderful! I am glad humanity has reached such a time! But you said you're from 500 years in the future? How can you come here to the 15th century and judge me by your standards from the 21st century? For those in the future to look back and do this is, well, estupido.*

LAYLA: *So good and bad is based on the time you live in?"*

COLUMBUS: *That is a great question... Some things are clearly bad no matter when they happened. But for other things, before you judge, you must ask yourself: What did the culture and the society of the time treat as no big deal?*

Now, we could ask ourselves: If Columbus doesn't see the problem with slavery, why is he pleased that humanity will reach a time when it condemns slavery? And if he says that "some things are clearly bad no matter when they happened," why is slavery not one of them, and instead categorized with "other things"? But there's a bigger problem here, which is that the video falsely implies it took 500 years for Columbus's behavior to be seen as immoral. In fact, he was condemned by people living in his very own time!

First, let's remember why Columbus is a controversial figure these days. Columbus enslaved many of the native inhabitants of the islands he explored. In his own journals, he noted the potential of the indigenous people for slavery, suggesting that they could be easily subdued and forced into the European slave trade. Under Columbus's rule, natives who didn't collect enough gold were punished with brutal methods, such as cutting off their hands and tying them around their necks while they bled to death. He and his brothers were known to use torture and mutilation as forms of punishment. Columbus established the encomienda system, a form of forced labor where Spaniards were granted land and could force indigenous inhabitants to work for them, often in harsh conditions. This system led to significant abuse, overwork, and death among the native populations.[23]

Columbus was so cruel and despotic that at one point he was tried and imprisoned for mistreatment of the natives. In other words, even given the moral standards of the time, he stood out for his brutality. Columbus' behavior was part of the reason the Laws of Burgos were introduced, which put certain restrictions on the treatment of Indians by the Spanish.[24]

As historian Roy Rogers explains:

"Early modern European explorers, adventurers, and traders were not the crew of the starship Enterprise. They were about perpetuating a system of imperial domination and exploitation from Ireland to the Canaries and Africa to, eventually, the Americas. This was a European-wide culture which promoted greed, cleverness, ruthlessness and risk-taking in its ambitious men in order to expand the slice of the imperialist pie for a particular power and its vision of god, be that Portuguese, Spanish, or English. Certainly Columbus's imperial sponsor wanted him to open a new trade route to Indian and Asia but they also expected Columbus to extract (by hook or crook) resources, wealth (such as gold), and labor from the peoples he encountered."[24]

But it was *not* the case that the people of the time all treated atrocities as "no big deal." Take, Bartolomé de Las Casas (1484-1566), for instance. He was a Spanish historian, social reformer, and Dominican friar who advocated for the rights of indigenous peoples in the Americas. De Las Casas initially admired Columbus, but as he he became more aware of the crimes committed agaisnt the indigenous peoples of the Americas by colonizers, he became highly critical of the mistreat-

ment and enslavement of the native population. His most famous work, "A Short Account of the Destruction of the Indies" (1552) is a passionate indictment of Spanish cruelties in the New World and it paints a grim picture of the entire early period of Spanish colonization. De Las Casas says that the *"insatiable greed and ambition"* of Spanish colonizers, who wanted to *"swell themselves with riches,"* led them to treat the native population as "beasts." The acts he describes are deeply disturbing:

"With my own eyes I saw Spaniards cut off the nose and ears of Indians, male and female, without provocation, merely because it pleased them to do it. ...Likewise, I saw how they summoned the caciques and the chief rulers to come, assuring them safety, and when they peacefully came, they were taken captive and burned. They laid bets as to who, with one stroke of the sword, could split a man in two or could cut off his head or spill out his entrails with a single stroke of the pike. They took infants from their mothers' breasts, snatching them by the legs and pitching them headfirst against the crags or snatched them by the arms and threw them into the rivers, roaring with laughter and saying as the babies fell into the water, "Boil there, you offspring of the devil!" They attacked the towns and

spared neither the children nor the aged nor pregnant women nor women in childbed, not only stabbing them and dismembering them but cutting them to pieces as if dealing with sheep in the slaughter house. They made some low wide gallows on which the hanged victim's feet almost touched the ground, stringing up their victims in lots of thirteen, in memory of Our Redeemer and His twelve Apostles, then set burning wood at their feet and thus burned them alive. With still others, all those they wanted to capture alive, they cut off their hands and hung them round the victim's neck, saying, "Go now, carry the message," meaning, Take the news to the Indians who have fled to the mountains. They made a grid of rods which they placed on forked sticks, then lashed the victims to the grid and lighted a smoldering fire underneath, so that little by little, as those captives screamed in despair and torment, their souls would leave them."[26]

Bartolomé de Las Casas

De Las Casas isn't describing Columbus directly here, but there's plenty of evidence that Columbus was a monster, evidence you won't hear in a PragerU video. Remember: Ask yourself what is being left out and who is being left out? In this case, the evidence of Columbus's crimes is being left out. And the voices of those who were killed by Columbus (or who had their tongues cut out by his men, literally silencing them), and those who criticized his conduct, are being left out. Then ask yourself: Why are these choices made? Remember, PragerU's videos are all in the service of an ideological project, which is meant to convince you that leftists are crazy and there is nothing to their critiques of U.S. policy. Ultimately, these are battles about present-day policy, not just battles about historical figures. Conservatives want to prove that racial inequality isn't very significant, that wealth and income inequality are fine, and that criticisms of the police are unfair. They do this the same way they defend Columbus: by burying the most disturbing facts. It's your job to look beneath the surface, to question mindless patriotic narratives and look at what happens to the poorest and most vulnerable people in your society.

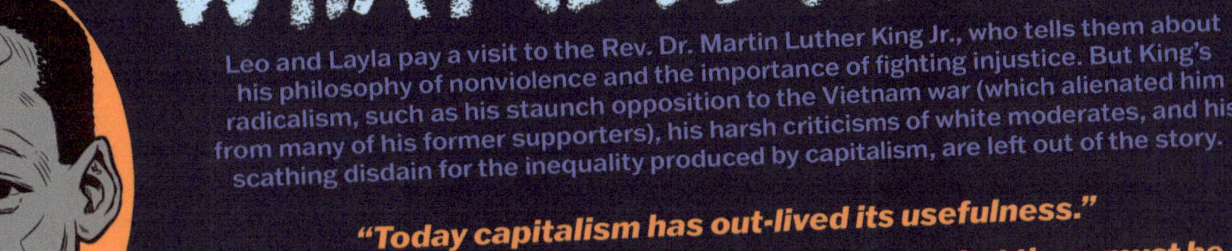

WHO IS LEFT OUT?

There's not too much that's objectionable about PragerU's videos about Betsy Ross or Alexander Hamilton. But always ask yourself: why *these* people? Why not others? What's governing the decision to include or exclude? Below are some fascinating Americans who you *won't* find PragerU history videos about. Ask yourself why not. Is it because they challenged ideological beliefs that PragerU holds to be self-evident? Here, find a few participants in American history you won't find profiled in PragerU videos. Look them up!

W.E.B. DuBois: A pioneering sociologist and civil rights activist, DuBois co-founded the NAACP and ardently championed the rights of African Americans through scholarship and advocacy.

Eugene Victor Debs: An unwavering advocate for workers' rights, Debs founded the American Railway Union and became a prominent socialist voice in early 20th-century America.

Thomas Paine: A visionary political philosopher, Paine's writings, notably "Common Sense" and "The Rights of Man," ignited revolutionary sentiments and championed democracy and individual rights.

Malcolm X: A transformative leader and advocate for Black empowerment, Malcolm X's fiery orations and writings challenged racial inequalities and reshaped the civil rights discourse.

American Indian Movement: A pivotal force for indigenous rights, the American Indian Movement galvanized efforts to address injustices faced by Native Americans and revive cultural pride.

Rose Pesotta: A trailblazing labor leader, Pesotta played a crucial role in the International Ladies' Garment Workers' Union, tirelessly advocating for workers' rights and gender equality.

Zitkala-Ša: A Yankton Dakota writer and activist, Zitkala-Ša worked relentlessly to bridge the cultural divide and advocate for Native American rights and identity in the face of assimilation pressures.

Elizabeth Gurley Flynn: A steadfast labor leader and activist, Flynn passionately championed workers' rights, women's equality, and social justice throughout her life.

Helen Keller: Despite being deaf-blind from a young age, Keller became an iconic author, activist, and lecturer, inspiring millions with her perseverance and advocacy for disability rights and socialism.

Clara Lemlich: A fearless labor organizer, Lemlich ignited the 1909 Uprising of the 20,000, rallying female garment workers against oppressive working conditions.

Dorothy Day: Co-founder of the Catholic Worker Movement, Day dedicated her life to championing social justice, pacifism, and aid for the poor.

Hubert Harrison: Dubbed the "father of Harlem radicalism," Harrison was an influential writer, educator, and organizer advocating Black self-determination and socialism.

ACTIVITY

Can you navigate Dennis Prager through the fog of his misconceptions to reach insight?

INSIGHT

"The few own the many because they possess the means of livelihood of all ... The country is governed for the richest, for the corporations, the bankers, the land speculators, and for the exploiters of labor. The majority of mankind are working people. So long as their fair demands—the ownership and control of their livelihoods—are set at naught, we can have neither men's rights nor women's rights. The majority of mankind is ground down by industrial oppression in order that the small remnant may live in ease."

— Helen Keller, socialist

AROUND THE WORLD

Around the World is an animated PragerU Kids show, and accompanying "educational magazine" series. It purports to profile kids around the world to show what their lives are like. In reality, most of the episodes seem to want to prove that the United States is the best country in the world, and convince children to accept conservative political ideology.

Consider the story of "Ania in Poland." There is plenty of non-political, informational content (the origins of the name Poland, a recipe for Polish cookies, etc.) *Part* of Ania's story is just about what her life in Poland is like. But the story takes a turn, and is soon about how foolish climate activists are and how important it is to keep burning fossil fuels.

It's all like this. Let's look at a few more examples:

PRIYA IN INDIA

On the surface, this video looks like the inspiring story of a young girl in India achieving personal success despite the social barriers imposed by the country's caste system. However, the video's description emphasizes its real point: "Through the life of Priya and her family, middle and high school students will learn how the British Empire lifted India out of a long tradition of caste discrimination. The narrator says:

"Along with advancements in transportation, agriculture, and government, the

WELL, THAT TOOK A TURN...

Family Gatherings

Every Sunday, Ania and her parents go to Catholic mass in a tall, brick **cathedral**. In the evenings, when she's not writing on her blog or chatting online with friends, Ania goes with her family to visit Grandfather Jakub, who lives in an apartment right across the street. When they visit, Jakub greets everyone with a warm handshake and a witty comment. When Ania offers him her hand, he follows the old Polish custom of bowing his head and kissing it.

When Michal or Aunt Zofia join them, then it's really a party! Michal drives his own freight truck, making deliveries all over Poland and Germany. Aunt Zofia lives in Krakow, and she owns and manages a café in Old Town that's been in the family since World War II. The whole community, and even the tourists, love it. When the café fills with people in the hot, busy summer, Aunt Zofia sells ice cream, and Ania and Magda put on their staff aprons and help out.

Page 8 of pamphlet: Fun facts!

have pollution like China and India...but if we stopped using coal altogether, would that make a difference for the planet? Those countries burn many times the amount of coal we do, and they're not cutting back."

Seeing that Ania was deep in thought, Klara smiled. "I wonder what your debate society would think about all this."

"I see what you're getting at, Dad," Ania replied, "but we still have to do our part."

Tymon nodded.

"That's fair," he said. "But did you know that in the two centuries mankind has been using fossil fuels, the Earth's temperature has only risen one degree celsius?"

Ania's eyes widened.

"I thought it was *much* higher than that," she admitted, thinking back to something she'd heard in class. Ania remembered her teacher insisting that without big changes in Poland's energy policy, Earth's temperature would rise by four degrees in the next 10 years.

Tymon and Klara listened while Ania talked about renewable energy. While they didn't agree with each other on everything, Ania and her parents listened patiently to each other. Later that evening, Ania sat at her computer and typed out an idea for her next blog article — will banning fossil fuels *really stop temperatures from rising?*

Was it possible that she had only been taught one side of the story? Should she have done more research before making big demands? She definitely had some work to do.

Page 16: Climate denialist propaganda!

British spread the influence of Christianity and Western values throughout India. They discouraged or even outlawed harmful traditions, especially those that affected women. When India was given its independence, the government continued to strive for equality..."

That's all the video tells you about British rule in India. You don't hear anything about the millions of Indians who died in famines under British rule, or the violence with which the British resisted Indians' efforts to achieve self-determination. The British were foreign invaders who ruled over the population by force, yet the only facts revealed about this monstrous tyranny are that it spread "Western values" and achieved "advancements." As Rudrangshu Mukherjee writes, "Whenever rebellion challenged British dominance, the latter reasserted itself through deployment of violence and terror. There was no attempt to justify and cover up the violence. Might was seen as right."[27] Shashi Tharoor, in *Inglorious Empire: What the British Did to India*, refutes the argument that Britain's domination produced "advancements." In fact, India's "subjugation resulted in the expropriation of Indian wealth to Britain, draining the society of the resources that would normally hae propelled its natural growth and economic development."[28] You'll find out a lot more about how the Empire really worked if you read the admissions made by George Orwell, who served as an imperial policeman in Burma (now Myanmar). Orwell wrote:

"I was in the Indian Police five years, and by the end of that time I hated the imperialism I was serving with a bitterness which I probably cannot make clear. In the free air of England that kind of thing is not fully intelligible. In order to hate imperialism you have got to be part of it. [It] is not possible to be a part of such a system without recognizing it as an unjustifiable tyranny...The truth is that no modern man, in his heart of hearts, believes that it is right to invade a foreign country and hold the population down by force...[I]n the police you see the dirty work of Empire at close quarters...The wretched prisoners squatting in the reeking cages of the lock-ups, the grey cowed faces of the long-term convicts, the scarred buttocks of

A BRITISH SOLDIER BENEVOLENTLY BRINGING TRANSPORT TO INDIA

the men who had been flogged with bamboos, the women and children howling when their menfolk were led away under arrest — things like these are beyond bearing when you are in any way directly responsible for them. I watched a man hanged once; it seemed to me worse than a thousand murders. I never went into a jail without feeling (most visitors to jails feel the same) that my place was on the other side of the bars...Not only were we hanging people and putting them in jail and so forth; we were doing it in the capacity of unwanted foreign invaders."[29]

Mention of this would spoil the PragerU view that the British were benevolent spreaders of "Western values." It might even call into question some of those Western values! At the end of the video, Priya wins an art contest. The "dirty work of Empire" is totally unmentioned.

READ BOOKS TO FIND THE TRUTH!

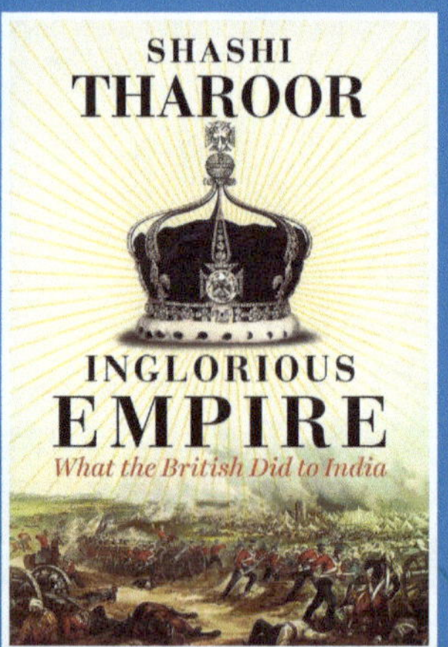

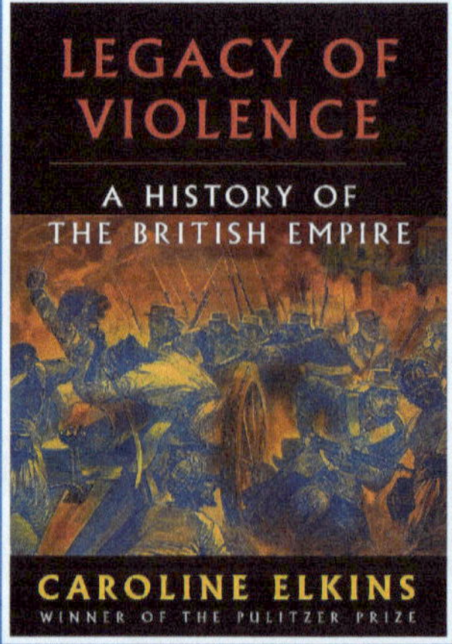

MARCEL IN CANADA

"Do your kids understand the true cost of "free" healthcare? In this animated Around the World video for tweens and teens, they'll follow Marcel and his family as they navigate Canada's universal healthcare system."

This video is an attempt to defend the United States healthcare system, by suggesting that Canada's government-run system would cause your parents to die of cancer. Marcel is a teenager whose father gets a stomach tumor. Marcel's father must wait for care because of the Big Bad Government in Canada. Marcel learns that "the United States is a great place for innovation, medical research, and new technology" whereas "in Canada, taxes and regulations make innovation difficult." He finds out that "Canadians make over 200,000 trips outside their country for medical procedures each year." Marcel's eventually moves to the U.S. so that his father doesn't die of stomach cancer.

Here's what you won't find out in the video though: because U.S. healthcare is so expensive, over a million Americans leave their country for medical procedures each year.[30] Why did PragerU tell you how many Canadians leave their country for procedures, but not how many Americans do? Because they're only showing you evidence that supports their ideological belief that government-run healthcare systems are bad!

You also wouldn't know from the video that:
- In Canada, 100% of the population has health insurance coverage, as it's a right of citizenship. In contrast, as of 2021, about 10% of the U.S. population, or 27.5 million people, did not have health insurance at any point during the year, according to data from the U.S. Census Bureau.[31]
- According to data from the Organisation for Economic Co-operation and Development (OECD), in 2019, Canada spent approximately 10.7% of its GDP on healthcare.

MARCEL'S FAMILY ARE PROUD TO BE CANADIAN BUT KNOW THAT ONLY AMERICA CAN SAVE MARCEL'S DAD FROM A STOMACH TUMOR

In contrast, the U.S. spent about 17% of its GDP on healthcare, the highest among OECD countries. Despite this higher spending, the U.S. does not achieve better overall health outcomes.[32]
- The Canadian system's administrative costs are significantly lower than in the U.S. A study in the *Annals of Internal Medicine* found that administrative costs accounted for about 34% of total U.S. healthcare expenditures, compared to Canada's estimated 17%.[33]
- Life expectancy at birth in Canada is higher than in the U.S. As of 2019, the life expectancy in Canada was 82.3 years, while in the U.S., it was 78.8 years, according to the World Bank.[34]

RELEVANT BOOKS:

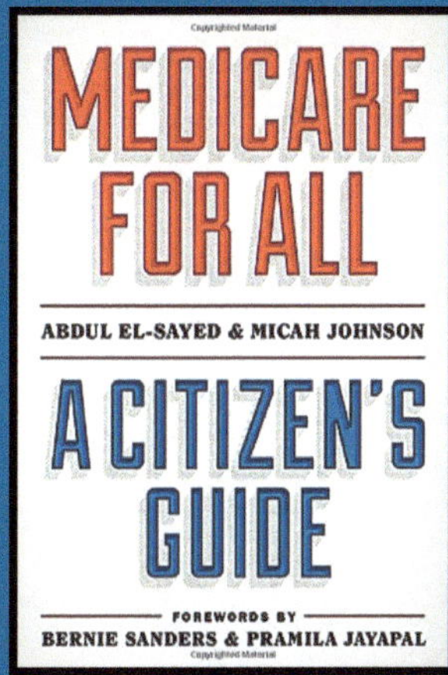

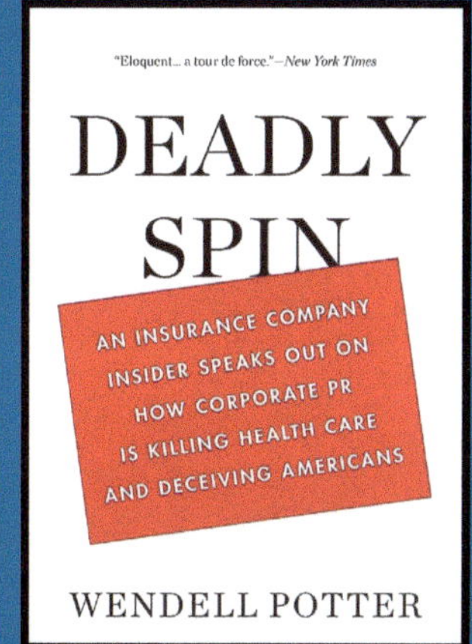

MATEO IN LOS ANGELES

"Mateo Backs The Blue" is a video about how Mateo, the son of Mexican immigrants, learns to appreciate the police. In 2020, Mateo and his family become concerned that Black Lives Matter protesters are threatening their neighborhood. A school resource officer, Officer Suarez, explains to Mateo that the police protect communities, and Mateo learns that protesters are wrong and law enforcement is good. Let's focus on an a particular quote from the video, to see how perceptions are manipulated.

"[In] May 2020, George Floyd, a Black man who resisted arrest and was held under the knee of a police officer, died while in custody. Although this happened in Minneapolis, Minnesota, fiery protests and riots erupted in cities all around the United States. Activists claimed that the police were targeting the Black community and purposefully killing unarmed Black men. As the false claims of racial targeting spread, so did the anger and violence."

Can you spot the many ways in which this quote is biased?

BLACK LIVES MATTER PROTESTERS HAVE DESECRATED AN IMMIGRANT FAMILY'S STORE, BECAUSE THAT'S THE KIND OF PEOPLE PROTESTERS ARE

First, it leaves out the horrifying truth of the Floyd case. Floyd did not just "die while in custody." A white police officer, Derek Chauvin, pressed his knee into Floyd's neck for over nine minutes, as Floyd pleaded for his life and said he couldn't breathe. Bystanders were horrified and so were those around the country who saw the video, leading to the protests.[35] The video doesn't tell you facts about American policing that led to the protests. In many cities around the country, police rough up, abuse, and even kill residents with impunity, and multiple investigations by the Justice Department have revealed patterns of serious misconduct by police that go unpunished.[36] There is a lot of credible evidence to show that police are more likely to use physical violence against Black people than white people.[37] Polling shows that 30% of Black Americans have said they experienced unfair treatment by police within the past year (versus 3% for whites), and while most white people say they have confidence in police, less than ⅓ of Black Americans have confidence in police.[38] Instead of considering the evidence, PragerU simply dismisses it by saying that claims of "racial targeting" are "false." Propaganda!

THIS IS GEORGE FLOYD, MURDERED BY A POLICE OFFICER

RELEVANT BOOKS:

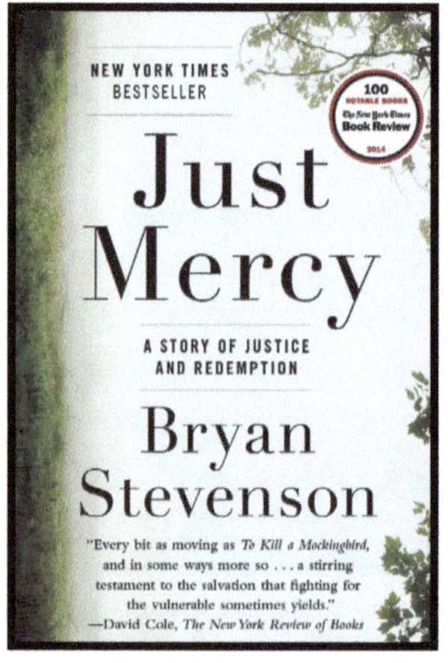

SHIRA IN ISRAEL

This video introduces viewers to the country of Israel by profiling a teenage girl named Shira who is about to start her service in the IDF. The video portrays Israel as a vibrant democracy that is sometimes attacked for seemingly no reason. The video makes the incredible claim that:

"Israel is the only country in the Middle East that does not oppress its minority populations."

In fact, this is a whopping lie. Israel keeps 4.5 million Palestinians under a military occupation that has been condemned by all the major international human rights bodies including the United Nations, Amnesty International, and Human Rights Watch.[39] Amnesty, for instance, says that "massive seizures of Palestinian land and property, unlawful killings, forcible transfer, drastic movement restrictions, and the denial of nationality and citizenship to Palestinians are all components of a system which amounts to apartheid under international law."[40]

In 2018, Israel shot hundreds of Palestinian protesters dead when they tried to cross into the territory that they and their ancestors had been forcibly expelled from by Israel.[41] PragerU portrays Israel's actions as purely defensive, occurring in response to Palestinian attacks, but Palestinian voices are excluded and you won't find out anything about the reality of the conflict. Read the human rights reports to find out the truth!

The video about Shira isn't PragerU Kids' worst piece of pro-Israel propaganda. That dubious honor belongs to the Craftory episode in which kids make a "DIY rocket blaster" to "learn about one of the world's most amazing inventions that keeps people safe: Israel's Iron Dome." The Iron Dome, we are told, was built after "thousands of enemy rockets were launched to attack innocent people in Israel." This is true enough, but once again note the omitted information: Why were the rockets launched? Why did the "enemy" attack Israel? The video does note note the vastly greater numbers of innocent people in Palestine killed by Israeli attacks.[42]

Remember: every oppressive country portrays its actions as purely "defensive" and treats the other side as the aggressor! So always look into the historical background of the conflict.[43]

RELEVANT BOOKS:

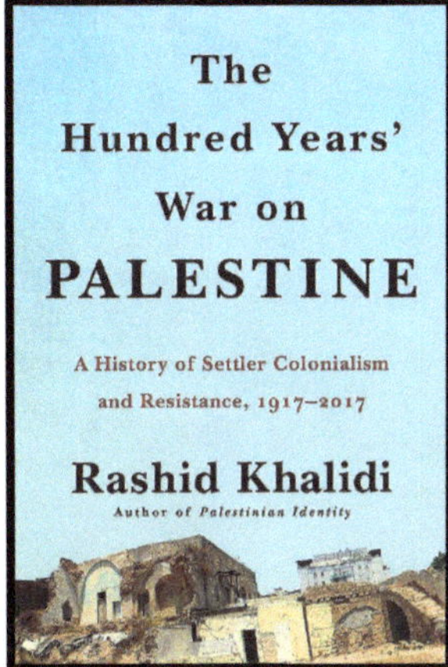

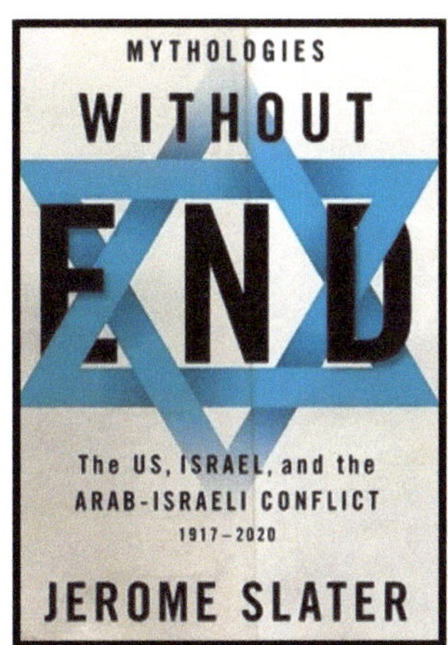

WHAT IS LEFT OUT?

PragerU's "Women of Valor" series profiles accomplished women from history. But they only choose women who agree with their ideology, and they leave out all the inconvenient information that may make you doubt these figures' "valor."

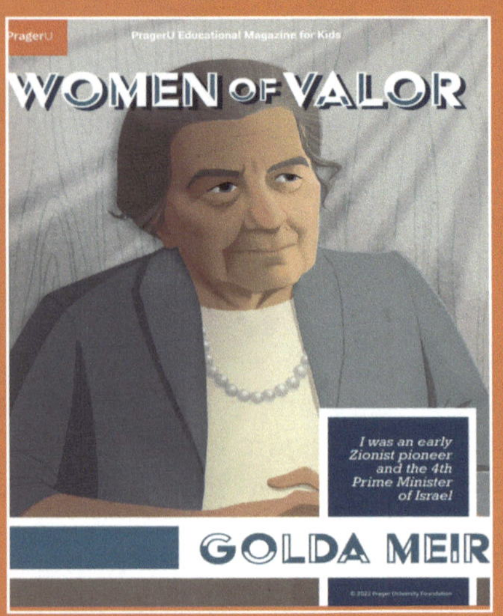

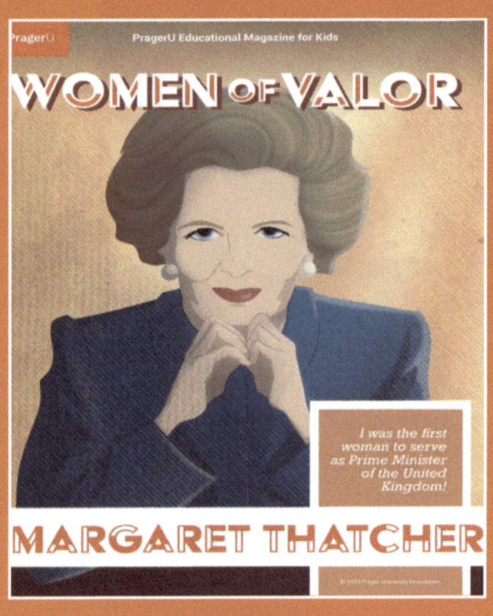

What you WILL find out:
"She devoted her life to the struggle for a Jewish nation, often at great personal sacrifice...Golda's strong convictions initially led her to Palestine to help settle the land."

What you WON'T find out:
"Settling the land" involved expelling 700,000 Palestinians from their land, and Meir became infamous for rejecting Palestinians' national identity, saying the Palestinians "did not exist" and denying they had been thrown out of the country.[44]

What you WILL find out:
Rand wrote best-selling pro-capitalist and pro-freedom novels and was an inspiring critic of communism.

What you WON'T find out:
Ayn Rand endorsed a philosophy of sociopathic selfishness and promoted a worldview that disdained any kind of altruism as immoral. She believed Native Americans "had no right to a country merely because they were born here and then acted like savages," and that for this reason, "any white person who brings the element of civilization has the right to take over this continent."[45]

What you WILL find out:
Thatcher "[revived] her country's economy and help defeat Soviet communism, earning her the nickname "the Iron Lady."

What you WON'T find out:
Thatcher crushed working people's efforts to achieve better lives through union organizing, made it easier to discriminate against gay people, and dismantled welfare programs, leading to drastic increases in wealth inequality and poverty.[46]

Remember:

PragerU wants you to think the left is crazy, and makes "straw man" arguments that misrepresent the other side! Read left-wing sources to find out what we really think.

Further Reading & Viewing:

Many YouTube channels have excellent videos carefully debunking specific PragerU videos. Here are a few:

- **Big Joel, "The Nonsense Politics of PragerU"** https://youtu.be/5uR-G4RB_Nvo
- **Shaun, "How PragerU Lies to You"** https://youtu.be/EM7BgrddY18
- **Some More News, "Kanye West, Prager University, and the Illusion of Free Thought"** https://youtu.be/hYAYFgmOWAI
- **Zoe Bee, "PragerU's TERRIFYING Parenting Advice,"** https://youtu.be/ZUz1nCRJJBg
- There are several playlists available compiling more debunk videos.

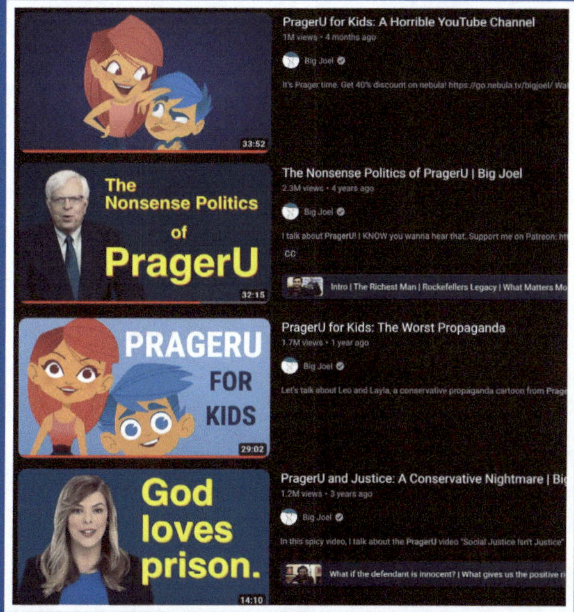

For a comprehensive overview of the left's politics, which refutes many common right-wing smears and misconceptions, pick up the book *Why You Should Be a Socialist* by *Current Affairs* editor-in-chief Nathan J. Robinson. For detailed responses to many common right-wing talking points pushed by PragerU, get *Responding to the Right*. Current Affairs magazine also regularly punishes essays scrupulously debunking propaganda. Get a subscription today!

htttp://currentaffairs.org

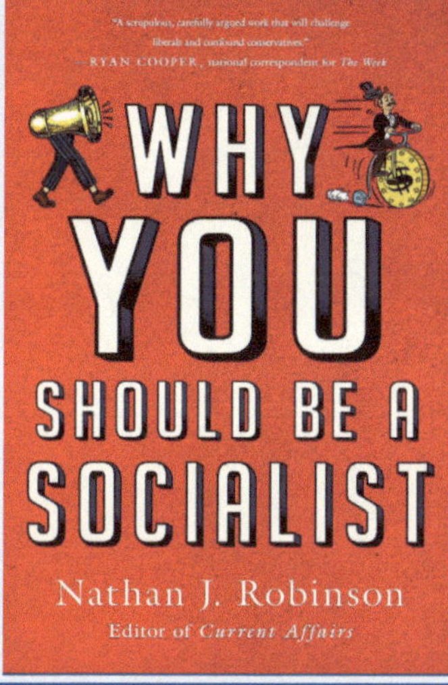

Notes On the Difficulty of Knowing What's True

by Nathan J. Robinson, editor in chief, *Current Affairs*

"I can't tell when you're telling the truth."

"I'm not."

"How do I know anything you've said is..."

"You don't."

—Frank Zappa, Uncle Meat

In the 14 years since I graduated high school, one of the most important things I have realized is just how difficult it is to figure out what is true, and how easy it is to accidentally find yourself believing something completely false. When we read history, sometimes we wonder how people of other times could have believed things that seemed obviously absurd. Until shockingly recently it was believed that babies did not feel pain.[47] Romans believed drinking gladiator blood could cure epilepsy. Sometimes, charismatic leaders can convince ordinary people of ludicrous and terrifying delusions. Cult leader Jim Jones persuaded hundreds of his followers that they needed to move to a remote outpost in Guyana and kill themselves with poisoned fruit juice. Hitler, of course, got perfectly normal Germans to believe that they had an obligation to exterminate millions of their fellow citizens in order to somehow "purify" their country.

It would be nice to think that we ourselves are smarter, that we could never end up being so delusional. But anyone can be fooled, for a very obvious reason: most of our knowledge isn't arrived at rationally. We develop our understanding of the world through trusting what other people are telling us. That does not just go for religious believers. All of us have to have "faith" that we are being told the truth, because it is impossible for us to prove all the things we need to believe. George Orwell noted that most people believe the Earth is round not because they have personally deduced it to be the case, but because they have been taught it. Orwell said that if we encountered a Flat Earther who asked us to prove it, many people would struggle. Orwell himself was somewhat confident he could deal with a Flat Earther, but less sure he could take on someone who argued, say, that the moon is a flat disc. Orwell concluded:

"It will be seen that my reasons for thinking that the earth is round are rather precarious ones. Yet this is an exceptionally elementary piece of information. On most other questions I should have to fall back on the expert much earlier, and would be less able to test his pronouncements. And much the greater part of our knowledge is at this level. It does not rest on reasoning or on experiment, but on authority. And how can it be otherwise, when the range of knowledge is so vast that the expert himself is an ignoramus as soon as he strays away from his own speciality? Most people, if asked to prove that the earth is round, would not even bother to produce the rather weak arguments I have outlined above. They would start off by saying that 'everyone knows' the earth to be round, and if pressed further, would become angry."[48]

Orwell was not here making a claim that there is any doubt about the shape of the Earth. Instead, he was making a point about the ordinary person's necessary reliance upon authority. We ourselves cannot simultaneously be astronomers, statisticians, historians, chemists, doctors, journalists, geographers, economists, and climate scientists, so we must all rely on experts to be telling us the truth.

It sounds perfectly reasonable to trust that an expert knows what they're talking about. A climate scientist knows more about the climate than I do, so if I don't know the science, surely it's reasonable for me to defer to the verdicts of those who do know. But what if I read two works by two people who both claim to be climate scientists, and they disagree with each other? Unless I take a few years off and try to get a PhD-level understanding of the subject, how am I to know which of them is right?

The problem is that when you're not an expert, you need to defer to the experts, but you can't always know who the experts really are without yourself being one. If two people show up and tell you they are doctors, and each says the other is a quack and a fraud, what test will you use to figure out which one is the quack? We know that throughout history, plenty of the people in any society who were looked to as authorities turned out to be completely wrong. Should the average person have listened to them or ignored them? It's a very serious dilemma, one that is not easy to resolve.
begin with.

People have to figure out who they can trust, and it's not easy, especially when lots of frauds are trying to pass themselves off as experts, so a lot of arguments between people are about who to trust and what grounds we have for trusting them. In Current Affairs, I have shown how many highly-credentialed and widely-cited people (psychologists, philosophers, economists, legal scholars, and computer scientists) can make completely bogus arguments that often look superficially reasonable. An "environmentalist" whose book is put out by a major mainstream publisher will turn out to be distorting basic climate science research.[49] A podcaster dubbed "the cool kids' philosopher" by the respectable *New York Times* will turn out to be dishonest and ignorant.[50] The respectable *New York Times* itself will publish totally misleading propaganda and treat undemocratic autocrats as the saviors of democracy.[51] A Nobel Prize–winning president who appears brilliant and inspiring will turn out to be oblivious and vacuous.[52] A smiling, charming vice president will turn out to be a serial liar.[53] Expert pollsters will turn out to be making stuff up as they go along,[54] witty, debonair public intellectuals will turn out to be racists who don't have a clue what they're talking about,[55] astute, prize-winning reporters will use utterly distorted facts in support of dubious theses,[56] and professional-looking think tanks will turn out to be completely untrustworthy.[57]

Personally, I am sympathetic to people who end up believing things that are very wrong, because I know how huge a task it is to sift through the barrage of information we receive and pick out what's right and what's not. (Worse still, some of the most reliable scholarly material is extremely difficult and expensive to access.[58]) I'm on the left, but I actually get why there are people who trust Donald Trump. Trump lies constantly,[59] but so does Biden.[60] Fox News often pushes dishonest nonsense, but so does the nation's Paper of Record. Often everybody on either side of a dispute is making claims they can't support. (Critics of the New York Times' "1619 Project," for instance, are frequently wrong (and the project itself is very valuable[61]), but the project's creators, too, have not been scrupulous. The *New York Post*'s reporting on Hunter Biden's emails appears to have been poorly fact-checked, but so were claims that the Post's reporting is "Russian disinformation."[62]) Never assume that just because one side of a dispute is wrong, the other side is right. Everyone could be wrong.

This does not mean that some sources are not relatively more reliable. The *New York Times* is not *Natural News*. The *Wall Street Journal* is not *InfoWars*. It does mean, however, that you can be misled wherever you go, that true words can be spoken on Fox and false ones by winners of the Pulitzer Prize. We can't be so cynical as to write off "the news" as too biased and untrustworthy to bother trying to parse, because ignorance of the world around us is also not an option. What we have to do is be vigilant and learn critical thinking, to demand that claims be substantiated and examine the evidence and arguments for ourselves. When we see a headline accusing a foreign country of doing something nefarious, we need to think about what it is they're being accused of doing, who is making the accusation, and whether it holds up. From World War I to the Iraq War,[63] the American public has been led to support horrific foreign policy blunders by treating the words of its government and its newspapers as if they are true, so we have an moral obligation to become "intellectual anarchists": demand that every authority justify itself before you accept it.[64]

PragerU has been phenomenally successful at getting millions upon millions of people to watch its 5-minute videos on political and economic subjects. Their videos are slick and professional, and hosted by charismatic pundits. They present themselves as offering pure factual information, and include links to sources so that you can check whether what they say is true. They may well appear trustworthy if you don't know anything about them (you might even assume they are an actual university, which they are not—this alone borders on fraud). But they're propaganda. They are not just "conservative." They are trying to take the world as it actually is and filter it in a way that will give you a completely wrong and false understanding of what things are really like and what is going on. They are messing with your head, psychologically manipulating you through extremely clever tactics.

That's why it's so insidious that PragerU is now infiltrating public schools, encouraging teachers to use their videos in the classroom as part of their ongoing project to slowly turn young people conservative. Teachers are not necessarily explaining to students that they should be extremely wary of every single claim they hear in a PragerU video; the *Huffington Post* reported that students in one school were simply being told to watch the videos and summarize their points.[65] There is research showing that just being exposed to a point of view in the media can make one more likely to believe it, because we tend to trust things we read.[66] So it's quite likely that putting PragerU videos in schools will indeed turn students at least a bit more conservative, if the videos aren't contextualized and presented as part of an exercise in studying different types of propaganda.

It's very important, then, that students learn how to think critically and demolish bad talking points. There is an extremely well-funded conservative effort to mold young minds, and because the left doesn't have any money to counteract that effort, we rely on having sharp and engaged thinkers. Learn how to spot manipulation so that you can keep yourself from being manipulated and then help others avoid being hoodwinked.

We have seen in this guide how an argument can be made for a position that uses real, reputable facts and sources but is actually propaganda, by which I mean that it cares more about persuading you to hold a political position than about giving you an accurate understanding of reality. Hopefully you see, then, how this stuff works. It's a bit like magic tricks: what appears to be the case is not what is actually the case, and the "magician" (in this case, the pundit) is pulling careful maneuvers to make sure you do not see what they are doing in order to mislead you.

Always carefully look up the experts you are hearing from, then. Scrutinize their records. Scrutinize their organizations. They will often come from organizations with benign-sounding names that suggest trustworthiness and objectivity. (Say, for example, "Current Affairs.") You need to use your judgment and be very careful.

What can you do about the problem of expertise? It's not always possible to evaluate a study to determine whether it has been well-conducted. You're going to have to trust that certain experts know what they're talking about on matters where you are simply less informed than them. What you need to do is try to test whether the experts appear to be honest and forthright, by looking closely at the parts of what they say that you do understand and seeing whether they hold up.

Some people have much to gain by misleading you. It's a basic economic fact that a corporation has a strong incentive, in fact arguably an obligation, to lie. Free market economist Milton Friedman said that the only "social responsibility" a business has is to increase its profits.[67] Well, a tobacco company's profits come from cigarettes. If the industry has reason to believe that if cigarettes are understood to be mass killers, they will be regulated, then under Friedman's framework, the industry has a social obligation to do whatever it can to distort public perception. Not only is it not bad to hire fake experts and smear real scientific researchers, but it has an obligation to do so! This is why the fossil fuel industry has worked so hard to throw doubt on climate science.[68] If the public understood the climate consequences of fossil fuel use, vast amounts of oil might have to be left in the ground, a massive financial loss for the companies. It is thus their duty to try to trick us. I once interviewed former Cigna insurance company executive Wendell Potter, who said that the major health insurance companies deliberately tried to mislead the public about the quality of healthcare systems in other countries. They didn't do this because they have an intrinsic desire to make Americans unaware of how much worse their healthcare is and thus suffer unnecessarily. They did it because they work for companies whose profits depend on the maintenance of the system in its current form, and thus it is their job to proactively try to make sure nothing happens to destroy that system. Potter was very blunt about what the companies do and the way that amoral profit-seeking is used to justify outright mendacity:

So: you need to look closely. Oftentimes, it is not obvious at first why something is wrong. You have to think about it for a while to spot the sophistry (arguments that sound reasonable but are actually deceptive and fallacious). Do not assume that just because you can't come up with a good answer to a point right now, it must be correct. Be a skeptic.

The world does not get better unless people work to make it better, and they can't do that unless they know what is real and escape from dangerous delusions. We have a moral responsibility to be intelligent. Look at the footnotes. Follow them and see where they go. Find out how people can lie with statistics and then teach yourself to spot the tricks in the wild. And always remember that nobody is too smart to end up believing something stupid—not even you.

WHAT'S LEFT OUT?

Many figures from history had radical political views that you won't hear about! Always question the stories you hear!

"[Capitalism] as it exists today is, in my opinion, the real source of evils. I am convinced there is only one way to eliminate these grave evils, namely through the establishment of a socialist economy, accompanied by an educational system which would be oriented toward social goals."
— ALBERT EINSTEIN, SOCIALIST

SOURCES

1. PragerU Annual Report (2022)

2. Jennifer Schuessler, "In Search of the Slave Who Defied George Washington," *New York Times* (Feb. 6, 2017)

3. "U.S. Health System Ranks Last Among 11 Countries; Many Americans Struggle to Afford Care as Income Inequality Widens," Commonwealth Fund (2021)

4. See Jillian Ambrose, "Most new wind and solar projects will be cheaper than coal, report finds," *The Guardian* (June 23, 2021).

5. For a good overview see NOAA, "Climate change impacts."

6. "Fossil fuel air pollution responsible for 1 in 5 deaths worldwide," Harvard T.H. Chan School of Public Health (Feb. 9, 2021).

7. Aryn Baker, "Outdoor Workers Have Little Protection In A Warming World," *TIME* (May 26, 2022).

8. Abrahm Lustgarten, "The Great Climate Migration," *New York Times* (July 23, 2020).

9. "Why is 1.5 Degrees The Danger Line for Global Warming?" *Climate Reality Project* (March 18, 2019).

10. Damage statistics are cited in Zofeen T Ebrahim, "'This will not be swept away': the bamboo homes helping Pakistan's post-flood rebuild," *The Guardian* (July 25, 2023). For the link with climate change, see Emil Marc Havstrup and Pieter Pauw, "Pakistan's Flood Problem Is Supercharged by Climate Change. Recovery Means Going Beyond Damage Control," *IPI Global Observatory* (June 6, 2023).

11. Kristalina Georgieva, Vitor Gaspar, and Ceyla Pazarbasioglu, "Poor and Vulnerable Countries Need Support to Adapt to Climate Change," *IMF Blog* (March 23, 2022).

12. See Nathan J. Robinson, "Climate Catastrophe is Theft," *Current Affairs* (Sept 4, 2022).

13. For a readable overview of the causes and consequences, see Greta Thunberg, *The Climate Book* (New York: Penguin Random House, 2023).

14. Geoff Dembicki, "How Fracking Billionaires, Ben Shapiro, and PragerU Built a Climate Crisis–Denial Empire," *VICE* (Aug. 25, 2022).

15. Chris Ciaccia, "UN report on world's oceans is damning: 'We're all in big trouble,'" *Fox News* (Sept. 25, 2019).

16. "Bernie Sanders: Candidates' Views on the Issues," *Politico* (2020).

17. Matt Bruenig, "Norway Is Far More Socialist Than Venezuela," People's Policy Project (Jan. 27, 2019).

18. Chris Weller, "Eight reasons Finland's education system puts the US model to shame," *The Independent* (Jan. 8, 2018).

19. John Logue, "Trade Unions in the Nordic countries," *Nordics.info* (Feb. 18, 2019).

20. Zack Beauchamp, "Australia confiscated 650,000 guns. Murders and suicides plummeted." (May 25, 2022).

21. Nick Warino, "The Data Show That Socialism Works," *Current Affairs* (Dec. 7, 2019).

22. The full text of Douglass' speech, along with historical context and an audio reenactment, is available on the website of the National Endowment for the Humanities. For more of Douglass' less-known opinions, see "Frederick Douglass Railed Against Economic Inequality," *Jacobin* (Feb. 202, 2020).

23. For an overview of the ugly facts, see Dylan Matthews, "9 reasons Christopher Columbus was a murderer, tyrant, and scoundrel," *Vox* (Oct. 13, 2014), Michael Coard, "This is the monster celebrated on Columbus Day," *Philadelphia Magazine* (Oct. 12, 2015), Giles Tremlett, "Lost document reveals Columbus as tyrant of the Caribbean," *The Guardian* (Aug. 7, 2006).

24. Dahleen Glanton, "Christopher Columbus was a fraud. He doesn't deserve statues or a holiday in his honor." *Chicago Tribune* (July 23, 2020).

25. Roy Rogers, "What *The Oatmeal* Missed," *The Junto* (Oct. 23, 2013). The title refers to a comic debunking the Columbus myth. See "Christopher Columbus was awful (but this other guy was not)," *The Oatmeal* (2013).

26. Bartolomé de Las Casas, "Brief Account of the Devastation of the Indies" (1542).

27. Rudrangshu Mukherjee, "Review: Caroline Elkins's History of the British Empire Is Indifferent to Indian Scholarship," *The Wire* (Sept. 28, 2022).

28. Shashi Tharoor, *Inglorious Empire: What The British Did to India* (Hurst, 2017), p. 222.

29. George Orwell, *The Road to Wigan Pier* (Left Book Club, 1937).

30. James E. Dalen, Joseph S. Alpert, "Medical Tourists: Incoming and Outgoing," *American Journal of Medicine*, Vol. 132, Issue 1 (2019), pp. 9-10.

31. Jennifer Tolbert, Patrick Drake, and Anthony Damico, "Key Facts about the Uninsured Population," Kaiser Family Foundation (Dec. 19, 2022).

32. "Understanding differences in health expenditure between the United States and OECD countries," OECD (July 20, 2022).

33. David U. Himmelstein, Terry Campbell, and Steffie Woolhandler, "Health Care Administrative Costs in the United States and Canada, 2017," *Annals of Internal Medicine* (Jan. 21, 2020).

34. David C. Radley et al., "Americans, No Matter the State They Live In, Die Younger Than People in Many Other Countries," *Commonwealth Fund* (Aug. 11, 2022).

35. "How George Floyd Died, and What Happened Next," *New York Times* (July 29, 2022).

36. See Ernesto Londoño, "Minneapolis Police Used Illegal, Abusive Practices for Years, Justice Dept. Finds," *New York Times* (July 16, 2023), "Justice Department Announces Findings of Investigation into Chicago Police Department," United States Department of Justice (Jan. 13, 2017), "Investigation of the New Orleans Police Department," United States Department of Justice Civil Rights Division (March 16, 2011), "Investigation of the Ferguson Police Department," United States Department of Justice Civil Rights Division (March 4, 2015).

37. Roland G. Fryer, "An Empirical Analysis of Racial Differences in Police Use of Force," National Bureau of Economic Research (July 2016), German Lopez, "There are huge racial disparities in how US police use force," *Vox* (Nov. 14, 2018).

38. "Poll: 7 in 10 Black Americans Say They Have Experienced Incidents of Discrimination or Police Mistreatment in Their Lifetime, Including Nearly Half Who Felt Their Lives Were in Danger," Kaiser Family Foundation (June 18, 2020), Jeffrey M. Jones, "In U.S., Black Confidence in Police Recovers From 2020 Low," *Gallup* (July 14, 2021).

39. "A Threshold Crossed Israeli Authorities and the Crimes of Apartheid and Persecution," Human Rights Watch (April 27, 2021).

40. "Israel's apartheid against Palestinians: a cruel system of domination and a crime against humanity," Amnesty International (Feb. 1, 2022).

41. Nathan J. Robinson, "I Refuse To Be Distracted From The Deaths of Palestinian Children," *Current Affairs* (March 8, 2019).

42. Niall McCarthy, "The Human Cost Of The Israeli-Palestinian Conflict," Statista (May 12, 2021).

43. "The War on Palestine," *Current Affairs* (Oct. 24, 2022).

44. Alasdair Soussi, "The mixed legacy of Golda Meir, Israel's first female PM," *Al Jazeera* (March 18, 2019).

45. *Ayn Rand Answers: The Best of Her Q&A*, Robert Mayhew, ed. (NAL Trade, 2005), pp. 102-104.

46. Alan Travis, "Margaret Thatcher's role in plan to dismantle welfare state revealed," *The Guardian* (Dec. 28, 2012), Andrew Kersley, "No, Margaret Thatcher Didn't Save the British Economy," *Jacobin* (Dec. 10, 2020), Harvey Day, "Section 28: What was it and how did it affect LGBT+ people?" *BBC Three* (Nov. 1, 2019).

47. Philip M. Boffey, "Infants' Sense of Pain Is Recognized, Finally," *New York Times* (Nov. 24, 1987).

48. George Orwell, "As I Please," *Tribune* (Dec. 27, 1946).

49. Nathan J. Robinson, "The Last-Ditch Talking Point on Climate Change," *Current Affairs* (Sept. 15, 2020).

50. Nathan J. Robinson, "The Cool Kid's Philosopher," *Current Affairs* (Dec. 1, 2017).

51. Nathan J. Robinson, "Propaganda 101: How to Defend a Massacre," *Current Affairs* (May 21, 2018), Nathan J. Robinson, "Lessons From The Bolivian Coup," *Current Affairs* (Nov. 27, 2019).

52. Nathan J. Robinson, "Obama's Words," *Current Affairs* (Oct. 9, 2020).

53. Nathan J. Robinson, "Democrats, You Really Do Not Want to Nominate Joe Biden," *Current Affairs* (March 7, 2020).

54. Nathan J. Robinson, "Why You Should Never, Ever Listen To Nate Silver," *Current Affairs* (Dec. 29, 2016).

55. Nathan J. Robinson, "How To Be a Respectable Public Intellectual," *Current Affairs* (Sept. 10, 2020).

56. Nathan J. Robinson, "Has the American Left Lost Its Mind?" *Current Affairs* (June 15, 2020).

57. Nathan J. Robinson, "Never Trust The Cato Institute," *Current Affairs* (Oct. 13, 2018).

58. Nathan J. Robinson, "The Truth is Paywalled But The Lies Are Free," *Current Affairs* (Aug. 2, 2020).

59. See Nathan J. Robinson, *Trump: Anatomy of a Monstrosity* (Current Affairs Press, 2017).

60. Branko Marcetic, "In His Lies, Joe Biden Is Sounding a Lot Like Trump," *In These Times* (Jan. 15, 2020).

61. Leslie M. Harris, "I Helped Fact-Check the 1619 Project. The Times Ignored Me." *Politico* (March 6, 2020).

62. Katie Robertson, "New York Post Published Hunter Biden Report Amid Newsroom Doubts," *New York Times* (Oct. 18, 2020), David Corn, "Giuliani and the New York Post Are Pushing Russian Disinformation. It's a Big Test for the Media." *Mother Jones* (Oct. 14, 2020).

63. Nathan J. Robinson and Noam Chomskly, "The Worst Crime of the 21st Century," *Current Affairs* (May 12, 2023).

64. Nathan J. Robinson, "The Power of Anarchist Analysis," *Current Affairs* (Dec. 5, 2019).

65. Rebecca Klein, "Videos From Right-Wing Site That Preaches 'The Left Ruins Everything' Assigned In Ohio School," *Huffington Post* (Oct. 20, 2020).

66. Mike Cummings, "Study shows newspaper op-eds change minds," *Yale News* (April 24, 2018).

67. Milton Friedman, "A Friedman doctrine: The Social Responsibility of Business Is to Increase Its Profits," *New York Times* (Sept. 13, 1970).

68. Naomi Oreskes and Erik M. Conway, *Merchants of Doubt: How a Handful of Scientists Obscured the Truth on Issues from Tobacco Smoke to Climate Change* (Bloomsbury, 2010), Kate Aronoff, *Overheated: How Capitalism Broke the Planet—And How We Fight* (Bold Type Books, 2021).

69. "Interview: Wendell Potter on How the Health Insurance Industry Manipulates Public Opinion," *Current Affairs* (Oct. 26, 2020).

Illustrations of Helen Keller, Martin Luther King Jr., and Albert Einstein by Nick Sirotich / www.nickelopsus.com